MW01200018

How to
Make Money
from
Rural Land Property

BY

Nick Maslaney

Cover image: © 2016 Nick Maslaney

Cover & Book Design: Vladimir Verano, Third Place Press

Edited by Jessica Levey

PUBLISHED BY NICK MASLANEY

Contact: land4all75@gmail.com

Facebook: www.facebook.com/nicholas.maslaney

ISBN: 978-0-9981222-0-5

I would like to thank Vladimir Verano of Third Place Press in Seattle for helping this project come to fruition. This book would not have happened without his careful and diligent organizational skills. Equal in task and importance, I would not have finished this book, as it is, without the careful editing of Jessica Levey. I am also thankful for the many dedicated real estate professionals, from realtors to escrow closers, who helped shape my views on many points throughout this book.

Although I live across the country from my parents, and have for many decades, their continued encouragement lit the fire for my efforts in rural land investing. My mother encouraged me to buy real estate. She taught me inclusion is better than exclusion. My father instilled in me the value of hard work, and passed on the belief that mental toughness contributes to better longer term outcomes. I am equally blessed to have two older sisters and one younger brother. I appreciate them more each year. With only five years in age separating all four of us, we had the opportunity to learn the benefits of positive cooperation and negotiation from one another.

Lastly, I dedicate this book to my wife, for her loving kindness to me throughout this process, and for being one of the most giving people I know, and to my son and daughter. Without all of their loving support and guidance, none of this would have happened or would have mattered.

TABLE OF CONTENTS

CHAPTER 1

Mission and Terms

THE MISSION OF THIS BOOK IS TO DEMYSTIFY and simplify rural residential land investing and to encourage people to look at this type of land with the possibility of generating income.

First, let's look at our terms. We will define rural living as acreage (one or more acres) that is 30-70 miles from a fairly large town or city, with the city or town defined as over 1,000 people. An investment is something that generates money, usually month to month, by utilizing a combination of certain skill sets, systems, and practices. Our emphasis is on monthly cash flow, as opposed to capital gains. Capital gains *can* occur, and are a nice encouragement, but the goal here is a monthly income.

Most people who try to invest in various investment vehicles—stocks, bonds, houses, mutual funds, etc—are only trained to think in terms of 'buy low and sell high'. Although the initial cost (the price of land) is important, as it is with many other investment vehicles, many times the terms are *more* important.

In addition, the concept of raw land especially encompasses more than stocks, bonds, or houses might. Raw land is an asset class that you can look at, touch, and improve. There are more creative possibilities with raw land (in regards to improving, developing, and financing) than with other asset classes. And though it's true that raw land as a whole is a great investment simply because they aren't making any more of it, not just any piece of raw land is a good value. Some raw land might not have been a good investment twenty years ago, and still won't be twenty years from now. It's important to know what factors to weigh.

If you were to ask most financial planners, accountants, real estate agents or investors about the best type of real estate to own, the majority of these professionals wouldn't mention rural residential land as something to consider as a long term investment, let alone an investment that might generate monthly income. But this book is not meant to debate which type of real estate makes the best investment, or which type of real estate yields the highest returns. Intellectually polarizing arguments of this nature are best left to the specialists, and many very good books have been written about investing in houses, apartment buildings, and various other real estate ventures.

This book is not another 5 step or 10 step program, not another get rich quick program. Everybody has strengths and weaknesses, is starting from a different step in the process. While many examples can be duplicated to some extent, there is no such thing as a 'sure thing' or an exact replication of results, as each property is different—each situation is different, just like all people are different. Moreover, the timing of each investment is different.

Buyers and sellers of property each have a distinct reason and motivation for their actions. What might work in some mountain states might not work across the country, or even be legal in another state, because each state has a different set of real estate laws pertaining to land. Furthermore, the examples given in this book are not meant to brag or boast, nor are they meant to demean or criticize anybody or anything. I honestly believe that humility is the best goal, whether we are looking at ourselves or at others. Failures and successes are best viewed within the context of our own humility, or lack thereof. Some might say a glass is half full. Others might say that glass is half empty. Still others might say of that same glass, that it's 50% contained. We can view these three perspectives objectively, not judging one's value over the other.

The mission of this book is simple: to show how one can create a steady monthly income from rural residential real estate. Some of the information given here might seem elementary to advanced students and seasoned warrior investors, but readers of any experience level will find the basics presented here useful in taking the next step toward investing. Wherever one is positioned in the food chain of information and activity, I hope to encourage them to improve their own individual standing.

CHAPTER 2

Advantages to Investing in Raw Land

MANY ADVANTAGES EXIST FOR RURAL RESIDENTIAL LAND as an investment.

The first big advantage is that rural residential land provides a basic necessity—housing. Many people who live in the country do so because they refuse to live in the suburbs or the city. And many people who have lived in the city, around so many other people, vow to never return to the smog and crowding after enjoying country life. To those people in both situations, living in the country serves their basic need for shelter best.

The demand for this type of living may ebb and flow, as does the demand of many other types of real estate properties. But with more relevant technology, the necessity of being close to a city has diminished for many small and medium sized businesses, and for their employees. People can now run a small business with just internet access and a good satellite telecommunication system, increasing demand for housing in rural areas. Enterprising people can do things 3-10 acres that aren't possible on a small 50'x100' lot with houses around everywhere.

Another benefit is seen for those in living situations with extended family. Small to medium size acreages work much better than a big home.

Rural property also offers permanence. Homes, including mobile homes, burn down or get blown over by hurricanes or tornadoes. Flooding destroys homes in many states every year. In fact, even a bad tenant can destroy a stick built or mobile home as fast as adverse weather might. Except for land on a hillside, or properties near flooding rivers that cause erosion, land does not move. Even in situations where a fire destroys the timber, crops, or grassland on a piece of property, the land itself remains.

In some places, a remote property suddenly becomes less remote when people start buying and developing the surrounding areas. In this case, someone who wants to develop his or her property may need to bring power across your property. This distant neighbor pays for the power and phone access installed across (or, ideally, along) your property line, and you get utility improvements without money out of your pocket. Because of the permanence of your land, the neighbor included his improvements on your land.

An advantage of raw land is that it affords the buyer, investor, or developer an element of flexibility and creativity. An investor can spend some money to make the land marketable to more people. For example, an investor who spends money to run power to a piece of land and then drills a well will suddenly have many more people willing to buy and live on that property. The same amount of money, spent installing a new roof and windows on an existing rental, will not reward the duplex owner the same percentage return on their cash. This is because the first expenditure is a capital improvement (a well and utilities), while the other is a necessary expense for the maintenance of a building.

Something else to consider: A larger property has the ability, in accordance with individual state and county laws, to be subdivided.

This potential can expand and duplicate wealth even faster. A big 40 acre property divided into two 20 acre parcels, or four 10 acre parcels, will multiply wealth faster than many other types of real estate investments.

Dividing acreage in this way allows for more creativity. Drilling a well on one of your properties and running water lines to a neighboring property you also own will increase the value of the second lot without the extra expense of a separate well. Increasing the value of a lot means greater utility to the end user and more money to the land investor. The same can be said of running other utilities, like phone and power lines. It follows that turning a large property into a mobile home park, RV park, or multifamily housing complex magnifies investment returns even further. If current multifamily housing already exists, adding another few units expands investment returns.

This element of creativity and flexibility gives rural residential properties a big advantage over other types of investment.

CHAPTER 3

Types of Rural Residential Land Investments

THERE ARE MANY TYPES OF RURAL RESIDENTIAL land properties. For simplicity, we will look at three primary types, and a fourth type that I call a hybrid situation. We will group the types by the level of development completion, or lack of completion, of the land. For investors, this grouping is important as each type has its advantages and disadvantages.

RAW LAND

The first type of land is what some people call 'raw.' Many definitions exist for raw land, but for our purposes we will classify it as land with no improvements, access to improvements, and no liveable structure.

Improvements are defined as water, sewer or septic, power, or phone. Access to these improvements is another consideration in raw land: Many times, power sources are very far away and not economical, meaning it will cost more to bring the power to the property than the property cost itself. This is in contrast to those times when power is only one or two lots away on a highway. Water access can also be an issue, as it might be very expensive to drill a well. No sewer could mean a very small town is not nearby, or a developer decided it was not worth the cost to bring the sewer to the land. Sometimes these raw properties are cattle or timber land, and no utilities are needed.

These raw properties are more speculative than other types of land, meaning the true value may not be realized until years later, if ever. They are long-term properties for off-on-the-horizon thinking. If we can use a baseball analogy, raw rural residential investing is that time before the 1st inning of a game, before the game starts. The players are in the field, but they are only warming up. Most spectators have not arrived, or are just sitting down to watch the game. As most people know, this is the least exciting time of the game—the quiet before the storm. With raw land investment, this quiet can last several years or decades.

This type of investing is for people who have vision. You have to try to see what other people might not see or want to see, something intrinsic to the property that will make it valuable in the future. This property trait could be privacy, great views, or valuable natural resources like timber, oil, or gas.

It is interesting to note that many of these properties have old logging roads instead of established roads along the property lines. Sometimes the old logging roads go through the properties, rather than along them. This is because when loggers log property, they are not paying attention to property lines unless there is a fence and a home to reference. While loggers have their heavy road clearing equipment on the property is a good time to make roads along property lines for future use. It is easy to buy a landlocked property with no legal easement recorded to the property, and even when there *is* a recorded easement, people will often use the available road and build their homes wherever they want to. When buying these properties, try to buy the properties closest to the main road, as these are the properties most likely to be developed with improvements.

Let's summarize the raw land issues and characteristics:

More speculative than other types of land.

1. Much potential long term. Can be farmland or timber land, or out of the way property that people usually don't look at it.

2. Far away from cities.

3. Not usually advertised, or one land company owns the property and divides the property into parcels.

4. Can be a high return, from any combination of factors intrinsic to the property (e.g. timber/crops/location/oil/gas/water).

5. Not as many buyers, or the pool of buyers is greatly reduced.

SEMI-IMPROVED LAND

The next type of land is what I call 'semi-improved.' 'Semi-improved' means one or more improvements exist on the property, or that access to these improvements is adjacent to the property. Once again, improvements are: power, phone, septic or sewer, well or water sources. These improvements do not include housing.

Many variations exist within properties that are called semi-improved. A property with a power pole or phone line running along the property line is considered semi-improved, as are those with power poles across the street or adjacent to the subject property. Either of these qualifies as improvements, if the power or phone is legally accessible—meaning that no written permission from a property owner or Homeowners Association is needed to develop the utility. To return to our baseball analogy, semi-improved land is the 2nd to 3rd inning of the game. Things are happening, but it's still early.

When assessing whether a property is raw or semi-improved, it is important to be aware that some terms used to advertise the land may not mean what you expect. For example, many realtors and property owners will use the term 'power available.' If you were to ask a hundred realtors what 'power available' means to them, you could very well get a hundred different answers. So, in essence, this phrase means nothing unless clearly defined each time, by answering certain questions: Is the power access already on the property? Is it adjacent, requiring a written easement by the property owner granting access? Is it forty feet away, trapped behind a disgruntled property owner that is reluctant to provide a written easement? These types of factors are why phrases like 'power available' should be followed up on with further inspection.

As a good rule, cautious investors should look for land with installed power first, then consider options with power lines on the property, followed by those with power located across the street, and underground green power boxes are best when found on the same side of the street as the subject property. Because advertising can be misleading, don't rely on a realtor's, property owner's, or anyone else's statement—make a visual inspection of each property yourself.

When considering water related improvements, many factors need to be considered. Is there a well on the property? If so, how many gallons per minute does it produce? What formations are in the well? Is the well drilled and cased all the way, such as a sand and gravel formation, or is it an open well, such as a basalt or granite formation? How deep is it? Has the water purity been tested lately? When was it drilled? Is the driller still in business? This last question is important because many well drillers don't want to make repairs on work they didn't complete themselves.

If water improvements include a community well or use of a community water system instead, another set of considerations is needed. In these instances, a sound legal agreement is all-important, as this determines the who, what, where, why and how regarding the way the water is shared, and how the costs will be pro-rated to each user. If the water system is provided by a small town, borough, or other type of community, the local governing county should be contacted to best understand the water rules. Variations will exist. For example, some communities will charge property owners for having a water outlet on the property even if no water is being used.. Understanding provisions like this is a must in determine the value of individual improvements on a property, and should be investigated before buying.

Another improvement that causes a property to be considered 'semi-improved' is phone line access. As crazy as it sounds, just having phone boxes along the property line doesn't guarantee a phone line can be accessed. Sometimes a phone company won't have run enough lines to service all of the properties bordering the phone boxes. Another few lines may need to be dug, excavated, and hooked up to the main junction box several boxes (and several properties) over before access is really available. Once again, it's important not to assume a phone utility is available just because an agent or seller says that a phone box is nearby. It's best to contact the phone company yourself for up to date information.

Like water related improvements, phone improvements are most valuable when a phone box is located alongside the property you are interested in. However, with the advancement of communication technologies, from cell phones to satellite dishes, land lines are becoming less important.

The next improvement to consider is the presence of a septic system or independent sewer system. Assessing a semi-improved property with a septic system involves many things. Is there already a completed septic system on the property? Perc holes (holes that are dug 4-6 feet in diameter on a property and used to determine the type of septic system to be used), might be dug already, or may need to be dug in the future. If there is work to be done, a finished site plan with county approval of a specific type of septic system is preferred. Once approved, are there dates that the septic system must be installed by? It is also important to determine the type of soil in the area. For example, if the area is primarily loam, sand, or gravel, there is a good chance that the septic system needed will be a gravity system. If a tank is already on the property, it does not mean it is legal or functional. If a system has been approved by the county, and time has been allotted for installment, costs can still be substantial depending on the type of system approved. In these instances, an investor will want to call a septic installer for a quote and cost comparison.

The last improvement which may qualify a piece of land as semi-improved is a driveway or roadway. While some may not consider this an improvement, for our purposes it is a factor in weighing the value of a property. If a driveway is not present, then a determination must be met mentally on the ease and expense of creating one. If a property can't be accessed by a normal car or pickup truck, the expense of a driveway can be substantial, and will effect the costs of continuing to improve the property. One may need a permit, or there might be a road association who owns access to all local properties (including yours). There might be restrictions limiting the type and size of a driveway. Because driveways, or the ease of creating one, can influence the ease of all other improvements, it is an important factor to consider.

Let's summarize a semi-improved property's characteristics and issues:

1. One or more improvements have been completed already.

2. Usually more permanent homes and living arrangements are allowed in the area.

3. There is more activity on the surrounding properties, more people are involved in improving their own or another's property.

4. This is 2nd to 3rd inning timing, the baseball game is just getting started.

5. Sometimes a buyer will need to finish or add to the improvements.

6. There is a greater pool of buyers for this type of property, from the casual recreational land users to the person who is going to build a home, or place a manufactured home, on the property.

Fully Developed

The next type property we will look at is land that is fully developed. I define a 'fully developed' rural property as one in which all the utilities are in and useable. In addition, a home is already there, or a mobile home is ready to be placed there.

With this type of property, there are more factors to consider and to validate. More work is needed initially to determine the accuracy of the utilities.

If there is a well, well log searches or well log data is essential to ascertain the accuracy of the data. Even if the well has been drilled for many years, it is important to make sure it is really on the property. Don't assume it's there, or listen in blind loyalty to real estate agents that say a well is definitely on the property. See for yourself.

If the property has a shared water agreement, read the agreement thoroughly to find out what it says and doesn't say. If the water is public (government or private entity), verify the regulations, charges, and costs. Check for water liens on the property from prior property owners.

If the property has a septic system, inquire about the last time it was pumped. Before putting it back in use, have it pumped if it is questionable or hasn't been done recently. If the property has a public sewer connection, make sure it is still connected and still works.

If the property has a working meter and power connection, the power should be turned off. Make no assumptions. Call the power company to be sure. The same principle applies for validating phone service—determine if there is a live phone jack servicing the property.

Let's summarize the factors affecting a fully developed property:

1. There are more uses for the property and a much wider marketability to all people. Many more people will buy a fully developed property than a raw, undeveloped, or semi-improved property. Everybody, from a farmer to a mechanic, could be a potential buyer.

2. Much easier to sell/finance these properties, and more flexibility in writing finance terms.

3. Buyers are more stable because they want to settle (nest). Less speculative.

4. Returns and cash flows are more consistent.

5. The entrance costs are more, developing costs are more, and the yield/cash % returned is usually less but more consistent. Client is better.

Hybrid Land

As mentioned at the start of this section, there is a fourth kind of property called 'hybrid land.' This type of property can develop over time or develop immediately. As you cultivate certain skills and talents, hybrid land becomes a very profitable and balanced approach.

This land is called 'hybrid' because there is a combination of factors and personnel working to accomplish a certain task. With a combination of capital and expertise, the land gets improved to become a more useable product. This type of activity involves the most creativity, the most 'out of the box' thinking, and should be used only by very experienced and creative people. Also, working in this type of land involves a high level of communication, trust, and respect between the people involved, ensuring all parties understand and accept their responsibilities. Many times, this format includes a written partnership between the seller, owner and developer, and the purchaser.

An example of this type of circumstance might be as follows: A seller will lease option a property to a buyer, with power and phone available. The seller provides a buyer with the funds to finish a well, septic, power, or phone installation, with an agreement to increased monthly payments or a higher overall land price, or a combination of these options. In another example, maybe the seller provides the funds and expertise to construct a well or septic system, while the buyer finishes the electrical work and provides their own funds for a well. In a similar example from my own experience, we (as sellers) paid to install a septic system and driveway, while the buyers paid for the well and to place their home with their own money. In these cases, a seller spends some funds, and a buyer spends some funds. Each assumes some risk while working toward a more finished product.

Another combination of options may include leasing the land and its improvements to a renter. This allows a property to be developed gradually. In this variation, the seller/developer/owner of the property spends the funds and assumes most of the risk. Rent can be adjusted appropriately, increased every year or two gradually as improvements are made, in order to get a better return. The property can then be sold several years later for a higher price, after all of the improvements are there.

Sometimes a purchaser assumes the majority of risks when working with hybrid situations, and spends his or her funds instead of relying on funds provided by a developer or seller. As a personal example: We once sold a parcel of land to someone with experience developing land. This buyer drilled his own well, ran power and phone to the property, put a septic system in, and placed a nice mobile home on the property. We assumed no risk in this situation, and it was a good case of full risk transference.

Chapter 4

The Five Point System

I USE A FIVE POINT SYSTEM FOR EVALUATING rural residential property, which corresponds to the five main items to be considered. Each of these five items is ranked individually, and when the score for each is totaled will create a cumulative score, up to 100 points. A cumulative score of 70-100 indicates a good buy, with 80 and up signifying a *very* good buy. A score of less than 55 is to be avoided or considered more speculative. Each item is worth a maximum of 20 points. The goal is to have a uniformly high score for each category. For example, some areas might score better than others, and a more uniform ranking of 16 in each category will show a better investment than a property that scores a 19 or 20 for one item and only a 12 for another.

The top point of the five point star represents access, the right point represents layout, the left point represents location, bottom left point represents development potential and the last point, at the bottom right, represents price. If you turn the star around clockwise or counterclockwise, it still looks the same, like a star. This principle is the same as our outlook on the land, all points are valuable. You want uniformity as much as possible. Although each item has its own strengths and weaknesses individually, all items are ultimately related. As an example of this relationship, consider a property with a great initial price, that takes thousands of dollars in legal fees and many years to settle an easement. These factors do not necessarily offset each other.

Each of these five items is necessary and important. Some properties are more important than others, or hold more weight than a mere 80 point tally. A cumulative score reflecting a combination of the various items will give a more comprehensive assessment than would only looking over a few factors, as some qualities may appear to be very good at first, only to change drastically in light of other areas of business, or the influence of landowners and governments in the future.

Let's review each of the five points of the star more thoroughly.

ACCESS TO PROPERTY

'Access' to a property is initially defined as whether you can drive or walk onto the property. Although this definition is an oversimplification, it's a good starting point. It goes without saying that being able to simply drive onto to a property will not always be enough, and does not eliminate the need for further evaluation. Understanding access to the property will start with reviewing a plat—a map indicating the divisions of an area of land, and showing roads (and what type of roads) within these divisions. A buyer will want to consider certain questions: Are these roads exact or approximate? If a road exists, is it found on the plat map? Most plat maps identifying roads usually approximate, especially those showing land divisions in more rural mountainous areas. It helps to look these plat maps to get a beginning idea of access. A great plat map should have a segregation date, if applicable, and include a survey. Keep in mind, even if a survey was conducted recently, various changes to the property may have occurred between the time the survey was conducted and when the property goes up for sale. People build homes, make fences, run power and phone lines on a property, etc, and all these things may effect access. If no survey was conducted and recorded on the property, arranging one would be advisable.

Access should be recorded with the local county to determine where the property owner can legally access the property without trespassing on someone else's land, and without violating water and other land rights while using their property. The local title company is a good resource for this, as they have plat maps, drawings, and surveys relating to the property, but do not take their word as gospel. Title companies do not guarantee a legal road, they only show a recording of what could and *should* be a legal access road. It is the same concept as somebody taking a picture of something and asserting a year later that the picture is still an exact match to the original object. In fact, title companies only maintain the 'picture,' the actual recording was done by a surveyor or land developer at the time.

Something that may happen over time is a legal issue that sometimes has to be played out in the court system. When somebody buys a property, the access to the property is usually exempted, along with other things, to protect everyone financially in the real estate transaction, if the property access is ends up being not what the buyer believed it to be.

To reiterate, when ranking this point on the star, consider that access roads should not only be visible while walking and driving on the property, they should be clearly visible on an aerial map or plat map. If no access to a piece of land is achievable by driving, meaning access isn't available except by means of a lot of excavation work, I would recommend not looking at the property. Why? There are so many other properties where access is easily obtainable. The last thing you want to do is get involved in expensive road building and driveway work.

If roads are clearly labeled, there are a few things to consider, as many variations occur. Some roads are classified as 'private,' meaning only those people owning a specific area can use those roads. Some access roads are shared with other property owners, and share access from a highway or county. In these cases, the county road access can either be maintained by the county directly, or not. A shared driveway with neighbors can be complicated if the documents are not clear and recorded correctly. If roads go through the middle of several properties, like they will with many mountain and remote rural properties, expect many challenges and disagreements. Expect sometimes reclusive and recalcitrant property owners to block other owners from sharing access roads that run through their properties. Highways or well maintained county roads provide the least amount of drama and other challenges.

As with all other areas of purchase, do not rely on a real estate agent, closing agent, or title person's opinion when evaluating the legal access to a property. When in doubt, consult good real estate legal counsel. Access to a property is very important, because it determines so many other things relating to the property that most people don't think about. These important subtle things relate to how a property is developed. Great access to an otherwise average property can add to the overall property value. On the other hand, the value of a great property suffers when access is bad.

LAYOUT OF PROPERTY

The next point on the star evaluates the layout of a property, which can represent a significant part of the value of a property. When the term 'layout of the property,' is used, it refers to the dimensions of the property in feet and its orientation to the surrounding land. What does the property look like on a plat or aerial map? Is the property a triangle, rectangle, or square shape? If the property is rectangular, is it proportional? Are the dimensions 200 feet wide by 300 feet long, or 100 feet wide by 600 feet long?

In general, a more proportional property (like one that is 200 feet wide by 300 feet long) is better than one that is long and skinny (like one that is 100 feet wide by a 600 feet long). Long and skinny properties are harder to develop and place utilities (like septic systems) on than are properties with more proportional widths. In addition, proportional properties provide more options for placement of buildings.

How level a property is is another characteristic of layout. Is the land mostly level? Sloping to rolling? Mainly level with gentle slopes? These examples are the main descriptions used. In general, mostly level properties have more utility and more flexibility— hence, more value. But a gently sloping property may be better than a level property for water or secondary water access, or to provide lake views. You see, there aren't hard rules for this. For example, in small acreage developments, steep slopes might provide a good barrier for privacy from the other properties. A pond or creek at the end of the property line is probably better than a pond or creek in the middle of the property, which would limit options. A driveway at the end of the property might be a better choice for utilizing more use of the property, but be a bad choice when bringing in the utilities. So evaluating the layout of a property depends not only the current-use plans, but also on how plans for the property might evolve into the future.

When looking at the aerial or plat maps of a property, look at driveway placement, tree locations, creeks, ponds, utility pole placements (including phone lines), and any other physical qualities of the property. Consider the legal precedents of driveways, roads, and utility placement, which greatly affects the property's future use and future value.

LOCATION

When one discusses the quality of a real estate investment, he or she usually hears that most value hinges on "Location, Location, Location!" This is definitely the case in commercial real estate investments, and is true in other types of real estate investments as well. But when dealing in rural real estate, we need to look at not just where the property *is*, but where it is in relation to other things.

The first location criteria we will look at is how close the property is to a big city (a city of 100,000 people or more). In general, the more people in a city, the more services exist to serve people living there and in the surrounding rural areas. There will be more choices for healthcare, employment, entertainment, and personal service businesses in a city of 100,000 people than there will be in a city of only 30,000 people. So in the context of location, it is important to find rural properties that are between 30 to 60 minutes driving distance to a big city. Some people don't mind driving more than an hour to reach a city, but being that far away will create a much smaller pool of people interested in a property. This is important, as a property moves closer to a city, desire and demand for the land increases exponentially. People like rural properties that feel rural, but are close enough to have "city services" if needed. A few miles to a small town might also satisfy this need, and our need to interact with people, so small town locations should not be disregarded.

Another aspect of location is the property's closeness to state or federal land. In general, it is a good thing to have state or federal land bordering or close by a property. But while most novice or lightly experienced land investors think that this is *always* a good thing, there is at least one possible disadvantage. This occurs when a property borders state or federal land and many people use the road bordering the property to access that land. In these cases, there will be a lot more traffic passing the property. If more people, hunters or casual drivers, pass the property, then the privacy of the property is compromised. Nothing can compromise the privacy of a property faster than rowdy, drunk hunters. This is something to look out for. A much better scenario occurs when state or federal land is across from the property, with the road divides the private land from the federal property. In this case, it is fairly guaranteed there will not be a home development across from the private property.

A third aspect of location considers how close the property is in relation to natural landscapes, such as hillsides, rocks, water, wetlands or other land formations. An adjacent hillside that cannot be developed adds privacy value to a property, because there will not be neighbors building a home there. Obviously, a property that is directly adjacent to a body of water is superior to one with only secondary access to a lake or body of water. A secondary lake-view property is still good of course, because at least some its view will be of water, and not a row of houses or mobile homes. A property that borders or is near a public boat launch is desirable, as it not only adds utility (being able to use a boat launch), but also an element of privacy, as the land is a natural break from neighboring houses.

DEVELOPMENT POTENTIAL

Of the 5 criteria used to evaluate the feasibility of a land investment, a property's 'development potential' offers the widest range of successes and failures. This means an issue the average person wouldn't think to consider can make a big difference, distinguishing average profits from very good profits.

When we look at the potential to develop a property, we evaluate the property from an individual standpoint, but we can also look at multiple properties, with the capability of scaling development to fit several properties. To determine the development potential of a property means to determine how the property can be developed to meet a higher use to the end user. A 'higher use' means more utility and more functionality, with the end (and ultimate) goal being to place any type of home on the property.

The first things to look to when evaluating the development potential of a property are the types of utilities on the property. As discussed previously, this is best done with a visual inspection. To review the four main distinct utilities to look for, remember that utilities involve improvements to a piece of land, and can include electrical power, phone, sewer or septic systems, and water sources from either private or community water systems.

Just as you would when assessing improvements to a piece of land, a visual inspection followed up with a call or visit to the power company servicing those power lines is recommended. The power companies will have their own aerial and plat maps showing power poles on or along property lines, and have an economic incentive to know this—the more people who use the power, the more money the power companies make. I touched on this previously, and cannot stress enough that the terms used in real estate ads must be verified and followed up on, especially when evaluating development potential with a five point scoring system. Many ads by realtors and private parties will advertise for land that has "power available." This is a misleading and potentially financially damaging statement for a buyer. If you ask the average realtor what this term means he will tell you one thing, a developer will tell you something else, and the average Jane on the street will tell you something else yet again. From my personal experience with this term, "power available" has meant that power is 200 feet away and cost $5,000 to install, as well as needing a neighbor's easement permission which the neighbor was unwilling to sign. As this example shows, it can be a big mistake to take a realtor's advice regarding the availability of power on the property.

In another example, I bought a vacant piece of land relying solely on a realtor's statement that power was available next door. I naively believed that since the power was only 60 feet away, it would be no problem to access easily. I thought, what neighbor wouldn't allow a 60 feet easement for a power pole and power line across his or her property? I spoke with the neighbor (who agreed to grant permission) but failed to secure a written easement, and six months later, new caretakers of the property would no longer accommodate my request. Long story short, the vacant property (without power) I bought didn't have power until five years later, when I bought the adjacent property myself.

These examples are meant to drive home the point that visual inspection of the property is a must, along with a survey done by a licensed engineer. When considering power access and its relationship with development potential, a good guide is this: Can I legally, without hassles and easements from any neighbors, contract with the power company to bring power to the property? Ask yourself these questions: What restrictions exist from local and state governments regarding power placed on the property? Does a small, powerful Homeowners Association limit installing power to underground placements, or do they consider each new case with a vote by a board? Many rural properties are not serviced by homeowner groups, which can simplify this process. Many people move to the rural areas for this exact reason—they don't like people telling them what color of paint is allowed for their home, or saying that power has to be run a certain way. Always check the title report and plat map for any existence of homeowner groups, and be aware that less formal, quiet groups might also exist among owners in the area. Talking to neighbors innocuously could lend valuable information on this issue.

The plat map will also help determine power easements on a property. For example, on many developments, power easements are recorded on the property's deed, allowing power pole placements along and on property lines, without needing each individual owner's permission. An ideal situation will allow power to be legally placed on the property without any interference, hindrance, restriction or encumbrance from any person or entity (whether private or public) before talking directly with the power company.

At the other end of the power spectrum, and something to be weighed when determining the development potential of a piece of land, is what some realtors classify as 'power installed.' Once again, this term can mean many things to different people. I understand power installed to mean there is a meter box with an amp service, and power can be turned on easily. To have power installed usually means there is a power pole within the property lines with a transformer, meter box and amp service. The meter box will generally meet an RV rated service to a full built house, covering everything in between. Be sure to consider pre-existing electrical liens from unpaid assessments or usage. If a past owner sells or rents a piece of land to another person, and that person leaves without paying the electrical bill, who is responsible? This is a good question to ask when buying, developing, and selling land with functioning power. Despite many alternate power sources, including solar, generators, and wind, standard hardwired electrical power is the most functional. The existence of power access (or the ability to get power to a property) has the most varied use of all of the utilities for a property.

Although I stress the importance of power access when understanding the value of a property, I am not fully discouraging the purchase of properties without power. It is just important to understand that these properties can prove very cost prohibitive. It is more difficult to develop, sell, and profit consistently for properties without power or with little real potential of bringing power to the property. To clarify, I would rather have two properties with power than three or four without power. They will score higher when tallying overall value, because they will sell faster, develop faster, and will generate faster profits in the short term and, more importantly, in the long term.

The second utility to review when determining the development potential of a piece of property is phone service. Phone service is the most ubiquitous of the utilities, and with the advent of satellite dishes and cell phone towers, old hardwired phone service is not as critical. If a hard line is desired on a property, many times the phone company has to run additional lines for that specific property, even if a green box is already nearby. A phone call to the local phone company servicing the property and contacting the lead engineer is always a good idea when evaluating this utility. This can also present an opportunity to ask about highspeed DSL lines and any easement issues.

The third type of utility to review is a private sewer or septic system. Septic systems add value, functionality, and usefulness, and should be taken into account when assessing development potential. In rural situations, unlike denser communities, there are no sewer treatment plants, and it is too difficult to run pipes in a uniform manner between properties like those in a community of homes. There are two main types of septic systems to consider: pressurized and gravity types. The pressurized system involves many tanks and electrical applications. The gravity type is a few tanks and a leach field. When evaluating a property that has a system, or claims to have a system, a septic installer specialist should be hired to determine the functionality of the system.

When evaluating a property with any type of home, it is not acceptable to assume there is septic system in place. Many times, in rural areas, a home is placed or built before the septic system is installed. Don't take the realtor's statement at face value, as agents are not septic experts. Their priority is to sell homes and land. The county will usually maintain records of existing septic systems, but the lack of a record does not mean the property doesn't have a system. This can occur for several reasons. For example, the homeowner may have self-installed a system, or it was installed before the county started recording in the area, and title companies will neither confirm nor deny a septic system on title reports or abstracts.

When evaluating an investment for home building, the soil of the area will usually determine the type of septic system chosen. A well-draining soil like sand or gravel will lend to a gravity system, which are easier and cheaper to install, so this will add to the value of a property. A poorly draining soil, or circumstances where there is a lot of surface water to work around, will involve a more complicated system and may decrease the overall value of a property. However, just because a septic system is more costly to install doesn't mean it reduces the investment prospect. It only means the initial cost is higher. In some cases, the soils do not perc, meaning a private septic system is not possible. These properties do not lend well to investments or developments, will rank much lower when scoring on a five point system, and should be avoided where possible. There are many other, better opportunities that do not have this serious setback.

The last and final utility to review is water access. There are three main sources of water on a property. The first is what some would call a 'community water system.' This system has water lines running to each individual property in an area, and an owner or investor will need to install a meter or water connection to the existing system. As a central water source, community systems can fall under private or public management, which will coordinate the water connections, manage the payments, and ensure the structural maintenance of the system. The main advantage of this type of system becomes obvious when there is problem with the water, because it usually gets fixed quickly. With many people relying on the water system, financial motivation ensures timely maintenance. Also, initial costs are cheaper than drilling a well. The primary disadvantage to this system is a lack of control for each individual land owner, and this can cause monthly water costs to get expensive. Community systems exist in rural settings where it isn't practical for each land owner to drill their own well.

Another source of water to a property might be a shared well, either sharing with just one other land owner or with several. This arrangement differs from utilizing a central water source in terms of size, privacy, and control of the source. With a shared well, there is a main well with several connections running out to nearby properties. There are dedicated easements from the main well to these properties, allowing for easy usage of water. Often maintenance costs of the well are shared equally, which benefits everyone. For example, if the well pump or well needs to be fixed, these costs are shared. Additionally, there is more privacy and individual control than exists with a community system. On the downside, more oversight is needed by the well users to ensure it is working correctly, with a good, honest well mechanic standing by for those who are mechanically challenged.

The third and final type of water system often found on a property is a private well or water system, which may include a tank filled by a private water company as needed. Private wells and private water systems serve only one property. This results in better privacy, better control, and usually better marketability to future clients.

If there is a well on a property, it is a good idea to determine its quality before buying the property. Many factors determine the quality of the well, including how many gallons are produced per minute, how deep it is, how old it is, whether there will be maintenance issues due to age, if a bacteriological test has been run to determine safety of the water, and the types of soils surrounding it.

As is true with septic systems, the types of soil surrounding a well influence its overall value. If the well has been drilled into basalt or granite, it may be an 'open faced' well, meaning there is a hole at the end where the water is sitting, with no well casing there. In these cases, a screen may be needed. If it has been drilled into sand and gravel, the well will usually have metal casing all the way down to the water source. In general, an open faced well is cheaper to drill, so if an investor wants to develop a property in this way, basalt or granite grounds will increase the development potential for the property. In addition, how deep a well needs to be drilled can result in lower or higher costs, especially in sand and gravel areas. A well log, filled out by the well driller, should indicate the type of soil, the depth of the well, and how many gallons per minute the well is producing.

Reviewing logs for neighboring wells can help provide an estimate for an investor looking to add a well to a property, and some states provide this information online. Calling or visiting the local well drillers in an area is a good source of information as well. Older wells won't have been required to submit drilling data to the state, so buyers of these undocumented wells will have limited information. With better technology, the well drilling outfit can still test the water purity and gallons per minute.

Another criteria to consider when tallying the development potential of a property is the presence of covenants. Many people think of covenants as mere aesthetic restrictions to a home, like what color a house must or the type of roof a homeowner must have, but they can have a much greater impact. In fact, property history in the

United States has contained many covenants restricting certain races from buying property in an area. These restrictive covenants are outdated and were eliminated by an act of Congress in the Fair Housing Act of 1968. Despite this history, age related covenants, wherein a buyer must be a certain age to live in an area, have increased in recent years due to an aging population. Demography determines many things, and it is especially relevant in property restrictions. Although many restrictive covenants exist in urban areas, covenants concerning rural properties involve other issues not usually associated with urban living. For example, they may restrict hunting on the property. If you asked the average suburbanite about hunting restrictions on their 50 X 100 size lot with home and garage, you might get a strange look, but developers must look for these rules and restrictions before deciding to invest in a property.

To further understand covenants, we must know where to find them. The majority of covenants attached to a property will be found on the title report. These range from house color to the existence of homeowners associations. Most people interchange the word covenant with the word restriction(s). Although the meaning is similar, there is a subtle difference.

Restrictions to a property, especially in regard to developing land, usually involve broad rules that are fairly common sense. For example, many plat maps attached to land will provide minimum distance restrictions between wells and septic systems—if a person wants to drill a well, a usual restriction will stipulate that the septic system be at least 100 feet away. This makes sense. If these restrictions aren't mentioned on the title report, the county will have a comparable restriction given.

If you are buying a completely developed lot with a well and septic system in place, it's a good idea to determine where the neighboring well and septic systems are. If you are considering buying and developing a bare piece of property, know where your neighbor's systems are before you start.. If no neighboring well or septic system is in place, it's a good idea to develop your property with your sights on the future, drilling your well at least 70-100 feet from your property lines in case your future neighbor installs his septic system near your property line. In addition, when you install your septic system, don't run the drain field and displacement field along the property line. Instead, run these toward the center, third, or half of the property. This makes for good neighbor relationships down the road, and if you decide to purchase the neighboring lot in the future, you will not reduce your options for future development. Other restrictions may include minimum septic tank sizes and drain field lengths, power and phone utility easements, a minimum and maximum size of dwellings, mobile home restrictions, etc. As a last word on restrictions: The topic is a large and complicated one that changes frequently in some areas. Experience, good legal help, and careful attention will help a lot.

Next, let's simplify the concept of covenants. When most people think of covenants, they think of onerous restrictions placed on homeowners in the planned communities of more upscale neighborhoods. This is part oversimplification and part truth. For this analysis, we will take a general approach: Covenants are specific rules placed not only the property, but on the owners of that property as well. These rules are usually managed by the homeowners and include written guidelines that are updated and revised regularly. With rural land covenants these regulations can address the land itself, like the kinds of trees you can plant and how high your grass can grow, or the home.

Many people choose to live in a rural setting to escape the tight regulations of government and city homeowners associations, only to find there are people who want to bring the city and suburb to the country and form their own rural homeowners group. In general, the further you get from the city and county seats of government, the less chance there is that a homeowners group will regulate what you do with your property. As mentioned earlier, a title report is a good place to check to see if a homeowners group exists, but it is not foolproof. Talk to local neighbors, real estate professionals, and other local professionals in the area to see if a new group is trying to form. From a historical perspective, homeowners groups were formed to exclude certain types of people, and in some ways not much has changed. Many current homeowners groups form to eliminate or exclude some form of behavior, in the long run excluding groups of people based on these behaviors. Often these homeowners groups masquerade as inclusive but the reality is anything but. If you decide to buy in a rural setting with a homeowners group, keep in mind that you will be subject to less freedom, more inspections, and more difficult building requirements. This may not be a good choice for a free spirited investor.

Price

Price is the final item to discuss in the five point system. Although the final price you pay for a property is, in this analysis, only 20% of the total ranking system, this area must be approached with a business-like mindset. When trying to acquire a rural residential property, the price you pay for the land will dictate many other present and future options. Two main prices exist for this type of purchase, one for cash and the other for set terms. In order to evaluate what makes a good purchase price or entry price for a property, we must look clearly at what the return might be when selling or renting the property.

Let's evaluate the cash price. Two methods can be used to determine a good cash price.

The first method is also used by realtors to evaluate the rental price of homes, and is called the 1% rule. For income producing properties like single family and multifamily homes, the projected monthly rent should fall close to 1% of the total price of the investment. For example, a single family home for $150,000 should be able to rent at $1,500/month. If the home will only reasonably rent for $900/month, the home is likely overpriced. Conversely, if a $285,000 home is renting for $3,500/month, rent is high or the home is undervalued. What one home is priced at is an arbitrary number, used to gauge the costs of an area. Obtaining data on the average cost of raw land and rural developed land properties in an area can be harder than it is for single family homes, and is usually collected by an experienced investor.

Let's look at a more detailed example of the 1% method. An ad describes a five acre property with power and phone available (meaning accessible) for $19,500 on the internet. You are just starting out in the business and ask somebody you know who buys and sells land regularly how much he/she would expect to make each month on a property like this. Your friend tells you that he completed a deal like this a year ago, buying a similar property for $18,500 and later selling for $29,500 on a long term contract at $210/month. Let's also imagine that the selling agent gave you the confidential information that the seller is moving out of the area and needs the funds to move quickly. You offer $15,000, to close in 3 weeks and they accept. When you resell on a long term contract for $26,500, for $200/month payments, your one percent guideline has been met.

Next, let's look at the second method used to determine a good cash price. Let's imagine that you are returning $2,400 per year, at $200/month.. If you divide this total into what you initially spent in cash, $15,000, you calculate a 16% return. This percentage is even better than the still respectable 12% you would make had you purchased the property at the initial asking price of $19,500, and so you paid a good price. This 'cash on cash return' is a better analysis than the 1% because firm numbers, not estimates, are used. This can be extended further to determine how long it will take to double your investment, with something called the rule of 72. If you take your return per year and divide by 72, the result will equal the number of years it will take to double your money.

CHAPTER 5

Case Study of the Five Point System

LET'S LOOK MORE CLOSELY AT A CASE STUDY of a property that scored high on the 5 point evaluation system.

PROSPECTIVE PROPERTY I

A 4+ acre property was listed on the internet for $40,000. How high does it rank on the evaluation chart?

CRITERIA I: ACCESS

I asked these questions: How is the access? Can we get to the property? Is the access route well traveled? Is the access legal? Do we need a tank to mow down trees to get to the property?

In this instance, the property was one street removed from the main highway, access was very good. The road was very level. The smallest vehicle would be able to access the property from the highway, in fact there was even a driveway. The road from the highway to the property was gravel, so the traction was good. Out of a possible score of 20 for access, I would rate this a 19.

CRITERIA 2: LAYOUT OF THE PROPERTY

I asked these questions: What does it look like? What are the dimensions? Is it a rectangle, square, or a landing strip?

In this case, the property was a rectangle. There were many big pine trees, and the lot was directly across from state land to the south. This meant no neighbors to the south, and the views were nice and very secluded. I would rate this layout another strong 19.

CRITERIA 3: LOCATION

The property was less than an hour away from a major city, 7 miles from a small town, 10 miles from a medium sized town, and less than 2 miles from a public boat launch for fishing and good boating. I would rate the location a score of 15 out of a possible 20.

CRITERIA 4: DEVELOPMENT POTENTIAL

In this specific property, all improvements (water, power, septic) had been made. The well produced 5+ gallons per minute and a 3 bedroom gravity septic system had been installed. Power and phone were installed, with power to the well. A 3 bedroom mobile home was already on the property. With all of these improvements to the property and a mobile home, the criteria score is a firm 20.

CRITERIA 5: PRICE

For this property, the price was $40,000. I made an educated guess of what I might make per month, about $400/month, with a cash on cash return of 12%. A 12% percent return means I would double my investment in six years. I ended up making $470/month, for a 14% yearly cash on cash return. I would rate this score on price as a 17.

The total score for Property 1 was 90/100. This property was a good buy and a good bet for stable cash flow.

Chapter 6

How to Find Rural Investments

There are many ways to find good deals on raw land sales. Here are a few ways that have worked for me.

Newspapers

Although the internet has replaced a good majority of print media, many people buying and selling land still look to it as their first source. I personally don't think it will ever go away completely. Many people like the feel of a newspaper in their hands, just as having cash instead of using plastic is appealing.

A lot can be inferred from an ad in a regional paper. Looking at an ad from a buyer's standpoint (in search of a good deal) means a few key points should be considered: How big is the ad? What is the ad saying? Does it look like the person took time to write the ad or did they just throw it together? Does it look cheap? (This might mean, "I don't care about this property, I don't want it, and I will negotiate down in price or terms.")

Once, I came across an ad in a regional paper that was only a few words long and looked cheap. This meant the guy didn't care about the property, didn't know what he had, wanted to get rid of it, or wasn't organized or disciplined toward the goal of selling the land. The ad was for 11 acres for $20,000.

On the surface, the ad didn't say much nor convey anything about the property. The only thing the ad revealed was that it was a cheap ad! To make a long story short, I went and looked at the property. It was 11 acres, divided into 2 separate parcels of 5.5 acres each and there were many older trees on the land. These were 30+ year old trees with good size and dimensions to them and I thought there was some good timber value to them. I found out that the guy had to sell the property because he was moving out of town and needed the money for moving expenses. I offered him $16,000 cash to close in two weeks and he accepted. While I did not have the cash at the time, my partner did, and I did all of the other operational and coordination details.

I logged the land several months later and took off $12,600 in timber, while still leaving many good trees on it. In this particular case, the timber needed to be cut or it would have lost value from the mistletoe and bugs destroying it slowly. It was good timing. We have rented it many times and have made our money back in 3 years after the timber sale. The land is now making $150/month for each partner.

The lesson offered in this example is to look for those small, cheap ads that most people are not looking for. They can be 'for sale by owner' or through realtors, it doesn't really matter, as long as the ads look cheap. These ads say "Please buy me, and quicker is better than later." When looking through print ads, determine what is the ad telling you by stepping back from it and looking at the bigger picture.

Realtor hand-outs and
Fliers in Stores or Restaurants

In real estate brochure listings, big money makers are not what a good investor will want to look for. Listings that provide the most commission to the realtor will be advertised first, and take up the most display. Properties that are cheaper, give less commission to the realtor, are harder to manage, and are more difficult to market and sell will be relegated to the back of the brochure. I am not implying this is an incorrect business move, as most people would do this. Realtors are in business to sell their listings and will try to sell an expensive listing over a cheaper listing. To the small individual investor or developer, this represents an excellent opportunity to snap up some good rural land properties by looking in the right spots.

One day, at a McDonald's in a small little town in north-central Washington, I decided to find out what listings were available. I grabbed as many colorful brochures and plain newspaper listings as I could, and went home to spend several hours looking them over. I browsed everything from single family homes to large multifamily homes and apartment buildings. As I suspected, the most expensive listings were in front with all of the great reasons why anybody should buy these properties. Since I was looking for the land listings, rural residential land specifically, the process became a little more involved. I finally stumbled on the rural residential land listings—in the back of the brochure. The ad that caught my eye read "10 acres for 10,000 dollars, with a creek, with power and phone." It only took up two lines, so the real estate agent had probably had a limited amount of space to fill out the listing.

I decided to look into this ad, and not just because the price was cheap. The potential value of a property with a creek, power and phone got my attention. I called the agent but the listing had expired, meaning the real estate agent's contract with the seller was no longer valid. I don't know if the listing expired soon after the agent listed the property on the brochure, or if the listing expired well after the brochure was distributed, and had been for a while, but it didn't matter. The agent gave me the phone number of the seller and I contacted them directly, and was able to negotiate a price of $8,000 cash to close a few weeks later. Eight years later, this property has returned not only our original costs, but has thrown off thousands of additional dollars and still returns a monthly income.

DRIVING OR WALKING AROUND THE AREA

Driving or walking around the area that you want to buy in is a very good way to find rural properties. Take your time. Turn off any distractions and focus on the mission.

Once, I was driving around an area looking to purchase a specific piece of land a realtor had told me about. This realtor didn't want to meet me to show me the property, which is a very common occurrence in rural areas for raw acreage listings. There are several reasons for this. In part, it is because of low commissions, and often the realtor does not know the area, the dimensions of the property, or how the property looks. In other words, many realtors that sell raw acreage have not walked the corners of the land and can't show a prospective buyer or investor the corners. Despite this inconvenience, this is actually good news for the investor, as the realtor will not represent the client to the best of his/her abilities, creating the chance for a better deal for the buyer.

The property was a 2+acreage, but I couldn't find it. I took a wrong turn, something I'm in habit of doing (I am directionally challenged, as my daughter says). I stumbled upon a *For Sale by Owner* sign, on piece of land that really caught my eye as it had just what I wanted at the time. I called the owner, made an offer, and bought the land. This property provided a good monthly income. After I partially developed it with power and phone I was able to sell it to buyers who finished developing it completely by adding water and septic systems.

REALTORS

Much has been written and will continue to be written about the value of realtors to the real estate transaction. Although not an endorsement of realtors, I will say that many properties would not get sold without the use of a realtor, because many sellers don't have the savvy marketing skills of professionals. Realtors have more contacts with prospective buyers (including investors) than most private sellers will, and realtors bring a perception of professionalism to the table.

In many cases, there are also distinct advantages to a buyer when using a realtor. There is a dirty little secret in the real estate business known as the 'pocket listing.' This is a listing that isn't on the internet or M.L.S. In other words, there is no contractual relationship between a seller and realtor regarding these properties, unless the realtor can find a buyer. The agreement is usually a loose one, and some realtors like these arrangements because they don't have to share a commission with another realtor. While on the surface it might appear that the seller has the advantage, since the realtor knows the seller directly and is representing them, many times the buyer has the real advantage because the seller wants to sell the property with a good price or terms. A desperate broker and a frustrated seller make great news for an enterprising land investor.

The Internet

Many good internet sites exist to help people find property to buy. The price and details of the property will be listed in the ad. Although many internet sites are realtor based, some are more neutral. The speed with which properties can be viewed creates a big advantage for internet sites over other methods, because a person can literally view hundreds of listings in a very short period of time.

The main disadvantage to this method is the general lack of quality information. Much pertinent information about a property is often omitted or unknown. If you are just starting out and do not know the area, this presents a challenge. Despite this disadvantage, many good deals exist on the internet if you take the time to be patient.

Tax/Sheriff Sales

Many states hold tax sales to collect unpaid property taxes. After a certain period of time, usually two to five years, states begin a foreclosure and create an auction for a property so that owed taxes can be paid. A good time to buy these properties is before they go to auction. Usually a good cash offer, with the buyer paying the back taxes, will motivate the seller. In these situations, the window to act is short because people change their mind quickly and unexpectedly.

DIRECT MARKETING

In many of the options previously mentioned, the seller or a representative of the seller initiates the process. With direct marketing, the buyer initiates the process by making direct contact with the owner or decision-maker for a property. Many, if not all realtors, use a direct marketing approach to solicit owners of a property to sell. If the owners of the property agree to list with an agent following this direct marketing approach, the agent gets a commission from the sale of the property. This commission is a one time payment, but when we talk about direct marketing to owners as investors, we are talking long term. We are talking about buying the property, developing it, and selling it on a contract for monthly payments. We want to get paid every month for holding the contract, this is the end game for investors.

Let's discuss the factors of successful direct marketing. To start with, this process should involve a very good understanding of the area that you are trying to acquire property in, and it's important not to send out letters to property owners with a generic letterhead. Most people throw these letters in the wastebasket. Identify what you want first and research it. For example, if you want to acquire a property bordering state or federal land, view a plat map, identify the properties bordering state or federal lands, narrow your search within these choices and then dig deeper. Type the corresponding property numbers and names into the available local government website to retrieve the property owner's names and any other relevant information.

After these initial steps, you can research individual owners. A few good suggestions for researching property owners are as follows: Try to find owners that are out of the area and look for long term owners with little history, indicating people that have quietly owned the property for years. Owners who are 'out of the area' need only be as far as a four to five hour drive from the property. When people do not physically view a property frequently, they lose contact, identity, and affection for the property, and may be receptive to selling. Finding a property with owners with little sales history will eliminate investors that have sold the property several times. A person or couple owning a property for years with no history can indicate many things, and you can state in your letter that you are not a realtor because many people do not like working with realtors.

Imagine you contact an owner with little activity using this direct marketing approach. He calls and you purchase the property 45 days later at a good price. You develop the property 3 years later, with some utilities, and sell it on a contract to somebody that wants privacy and no neighbors. Ten years later, the satisfied customer you sold to is still making contract payments to you.

This is the general process. If you know the area and become familiar with the properties you are researching, the direct marketing approach is a very powerful and effective method for acquiring rural residential investment properties. It takes some time and patience, but the results can be very good.

Chapter 7

Fragmentation of the Real Estate Industry

Realtors

THE REAL ESTATE INDUSTRY IS A FRAGMENTED BUSINESS, with many people doing many different things both independently and collectively as specific needs arise. The industry consists mainly of realtors, mortgage personnel (a group that includes banks and personal financiers who originate loans and notes), and escrow and note collection personnel (a group of people who close transactions and sometimes collect the mortgage and note payments). In some parts of the country, escrow professionals are primarily attorneys that handle closings and in any part of the country, most attorneys can handle any closings. Added to this list is another smaller group of support personnel, including home inspectors, property management personnel, appraisal professionals, builders (contractors and subcontractors) and developers.

This fragmentation of the industry and the specialization of each function has helped fuel a real estate bubble. This occurred as each participant became increasingly specialized, while also becoming less aware of other specialists' overall functions, and the functions of the entities these professionals represented. Since most participants in the real estate bubble and the real estate economy had no real skin in the game, each job specialization was meant solely to maximize each person's and company's profit.

In order to play in any game and know that game well, it is necessary to identify the players and their function.

Let's start with realtors. There are common myths and misunderstandings about realtors, the first being that the realtor represents only the seller. I am not sure where this myth started, but it's been around for a quite a while. If a realtor is selling his or her own property, this presumption might be true, but that's a rare occurrence. Even when a realtor is selling a personal property, he or she has other people to report to and rely on. In reality, the role and function of a realtor is usually very complicated and complex.

In the organizational chain of business, the realtor reports to a broker or managing broker. The Law of Agency, a written disclosure indicating who represents who, dictates that the realtor can represent the seller, buyer, or both. Despite this, the reality is often less direct. The order of preference and representation is usually that a realtor represents the broker first, himself or herself second, and the client last, whether it is the seller, buyer, or both the buyer and seller in a circumstance called dual agency.

This warrants a word of caution to investors: Dual agency is very difficult (if not impossible) to for any realtor to perform well. There is too much drama. The realtor is fractured in his or her representation, and often can't help but to favor one side over the other. One side will offer more or better communication, the realtor will personally know one side better, or the realtor will simply be interested in a commission and not care about representing both sides equally. In most cases of dual agency, one party is not represented completely.

The next myth concerning realtors is that they are knowledgeable specialists regarding land. In reality, there are only a few very good realtors who know land and land investments well, who know what sells and for how much. This is because good rural investments are hard to find and take time to develop, and most realtors don't have the time or patience to find them or even learn to recognize them. Additionally, there is much turnover in the industry, making it difficult for anybody to develop a deep skill or understanding of land and what it takes to develop, market, and sell it. Many real estate agents start part time and stay part time for years, only offering part time commitment. While difficult to work around, this reality does present a good opportunity for knowledgeable buyers to buy at good prices and terms from realtors who don't understand what they are selling.

Vertical integration

The goal of vertical integration is to get closer to the end user, either by eliminating an outside function or by controlling the prices paid for outside materials (as in a manufacturing context). Consider a car manufacturer; here, the manufacturer would like to control the price of a material essential for their success, such as steel, by owning a steel mill. This eliminates an outside function, putting the manufacturer in more direct contact with the end user, the car buyer. Vertically integrating your approach in the land business might mean choosing owner financing on properties instead of opting for an outside source of financing. Waiting for outside financing to purchase properties limits your overall flexibility and control, while owner financing allows for creativity in terms while speeding up the process. In down markets, this elimination of outside financing can be critical to survival.

Ownership and control of the system

Most professionals in the real estate industry, from the realtor to the closer, appraiser, etc, get paid only once when a transaction closes. When business is brisk, so are the paychecks and when business slows, so do the paychecks. But expenses are a constant for most people, whether personal to business costs. How can you address this challenge?

What I am talking about here is control of the system. When a real estate investor sells a property to a buyer on a contract or deed of trust, he or she owns and controls the system by controlling when he or she is paid (usually monthly). Like a bank, the seller of a property is in first position. By being in first position, this means most liens are junior to the seller. Many years after this property closes, the seller will still be getting monthly payments from the buyer. This business model is superior to only being paid once but it is also harder to build, maintain, and increase in volume. It is worth the effort.

Adding value to land through improvements, and partnerships

Increasing the value, utility, and functionality of land can be approached in many ways. One of these is by making small improvements. This can be done by adding a transformer to a power pole on the property, or adding power poles to the property so that the buyer can add the utility meter later. Other improvements include improving or adding driveways, phone lines, and internet services. These are small monetary and time investments, but will increase the return on a property in an enormous way. Some people may only want and need a partially developed property, or don't currently have the funds to finish developing the property, but there are high odds that a buyer will prefer land with power close by, more readily available, to land with no power.

EQUITY

Some businesses define equity as what is left over after the liabilities of property are subtracted from the assets of a property (Assets — Liabilities = Capital). This can also be shown in another form, where Assets = Liabilities + Capital, where capital refers to an owner's equity. For example, somebody with $50,000 cash in the bank and a car liability of $10,000 will have an equity position of (or capital in the amount of) of $40,000. This is what somebody has left over to spend, invest, or save. Many real estate professionals (agents, appraisers, bankers, financiers, and developers) claim that equity represents a specific number. These professionals have a stake in continuing the illusion of equity in a property.

Since our discussion is about rural land both with and without improvements, we are often trying to determine what a property is worth first without improvements, to determine its equity. We can look at several areas for a reference. County governments have assessed values of all listed properties, determined from items like past sales and property size. Real estate professionals can provide estimates based on current and past experience with the area. These two resources are not always the most objective, since county governments want higher assessed land values (which will lead to higher taxes and increased government resources), realtors want higher sales commissions, and bankers/appraisers want to make higher fees.

A third method for determining the value of a property is what I would call 'real time value.' What would the property sell for today? Who would buy the property today, and at what price?

Sometimes buyers believe they are entitled to equity positions when they have to sell, and will at times try to sell their property and collect the proceeds of a down payment without first paying the first position mortgage. This could be considered equity skimming (at the minimum), because most contracts state that any proceeds from selling must go toward paying the under-lining mortgage (or first position) first. Making payments on a real estate contract to the seller does not entitle someone to an equity position as some people might believe. When a property is sold, either by cash or on a contract, many expenses have to be accounted for. This is where the illusion of equity comes in, as these expenses can't be placed at the bottom of the priority list. Many people don't realize that a purchaser can pay on a real estate contract for *years* and not get any equity. Equity is an illusion perpetrated by the real estate industry to make people believe they are entitled to something.

To explain this further with an example, imagine a buyer owes $20,000 on a property and is secured by a first position note. He or she owes this much to the seller *first*. If, hypothetically, this buyer has a new appraisal done and the appraisal says the property is worth $35,000, what would the equity be? Some would quickly say $15,000, but this is false thinking. If this home is financeable, that might be the case, but for the purposes of this book, equity does not happen until the buyer sells the property, pays off the underlying loan, and has money left over. When we are buying, selling, developing, improving, and ultimately receiving cash payments for a property, we are not concerned with the term equity.

CHAPTER 8

Baseball and Investing

THE GOAL OF THIS BOOK IS TO PROVIDE THE TOOLS needed to make a stable monthly income by investing in rural real estate. Previously, we used an analogy between the 1st inning of a baseball game and raw land investing to show that working in raw land takes foresight. Let's revisit this analogy now in a new way, by relating baseball to the concepts and 'players' in rural real estate.

In any baseball game, from Little League to Major League, there are a variety of ways to win. To win a game, one team just has to score more runs than the other team, and to win the World Series Championship, a team must score the most runs in the majority of seven games. As a general rule, the team that has more hits, commits fewer errors, and pitches best usually wins the game. However, sometimes a team does all these things—outhits, has fewer errors, and generally pitches better—but still loses, because the timing or lack of timing doesn't turn those hits into runs.

To understand how to score runs and win in real estate, let's look at the objectives of baseball and the members of the team and how they relate to the concepts and personnel of land investing. As stated, the objective in baseball is to score the most runs and commit the least amount of errors. The objective when investing in raw, semi-improved or improved land is to generate monthly cash flow *first* and capital gains *second*. With that understood, we look at the various members of baseball teams and their corresponding roles in a land investing team.

The first member we'll look at is the Coach. He or she sets the tone on the baseball field. This is similar to the way that the mission, purpose, or goals of an investing team set the tone of the investments. The Coach is to the team as the Mission is to a Land Investor.

Next we look to the Pitcher. In investing, this role corresponds to the business model, marketing orientation, and marketing advantage of a particular Investor. It is what makes the Investor different. If we look at an individual on an investing team, this role corresponds to a 'rainmaker,' an instigator, an initiator of deals.

On to the Catcher. If this role is provided by an individual in an investing team, he or she would be the 'pitcher's' business partner, spouse, or associate. The catcher can at times behave as a mentor to the 'pitcher' if that person is inexperienced.

For both the Pitcher and Catcher, Instigator and Associate, interaction and teamwork are more important than their individual skill sets. Neither is more important individually. In regards to investing, the 'pitcher' and 'catcher' are the main movers and shakers of a deal. The pitcher is the instigator—looking, negotiating, offering to buy the property—while the catcher sells properties. This dynamic can be seen in other business partnerships, outside of real estate as well. Many great organizations had a 'pitcher' and 'catcher': Bill Gates had Paul Allen at Microsoft, Warren Buffet has Charlie Munger, Steve Jobs had Steve Wozniak.

Next we explore the players on the infield, the main support system of the team, beginning first with the Shortstop. The Shortstop usually has the best range among infielders, and corresponds well to the Escrow Department who handles closings. I like to think of a good Escrow Department as a very athletic Shortstop who covers a lot of ground and makes many outs (either by throwing out the runner at 1st, tagging out an attempted steal at 2nd or catching a fly). These closers can be called on to catch mistakes, ensure all paperwork is completed, etc. When an investor makes a pitch (buys a property), does the due diligence and homework, and tries to close, only to find he or she is missing documents or other key requirements, it can be very frustrating. In baseball, Shortstops should have the highest percentage of error free plays, and the same should apply to Escrow closers. A closer who makes repeated mistakes and misses a lot of pieces will really make things difficult for both the buyer and seller. An Escrow department should have an attitude of staying error and drama free, closing on time, all the time. Dealing with Escrow should be boring, dull, mechanical—these are signs that things are going well. This uneventful nature in dealings with the department is necessary for proper execution of duties, considering the tensions found between buyers, sellers, and realtors.

For our last player comparison on the infield, we turn our attention to the Third Baseman. The third base position is often called the 'hot corner.' I think of investing's corresponding position as being the Title Officer, or the person (or people) that handles the title for a sale. Sometimes a company will perform both escrow and title. Nevertheless, the Title Officer is there to prevent any potential problems in the future for the buyer or seller, making theirs a 'hot corner' too. For example, if a buyer finds a good land investment only to learn during a preliminary title search that there are no recorded road easements for them to use, this is a hot potential problem for them and neighboring land owners.

The outfield serves as secondary support for a baseball team. For Investors, this secondary support comes from attorneys, friends and family members who provide support and mentorship, and any other personnel who encourage and enable you to focus on your mission. A good Real Estate Attorney makes a good Center Fielder!

CHAPTER 9

Getting Started

GETTING STARTED

THERE ARE MANY AREAS TO TAP to find the necessary cash to start investing in land. The first step here is to sit back and evaluate your total financial picture. Gather, consolidate, focus, and build your cash reserves to invest. If you are considering starting with a bank or credit union loan, it is vital to remember that most banks and credit unions won't lend on raw land, or in many cases even land with some utility improvements. Banks view raw land with utilities as illiquid—something that cannot be easily converted to cash—and a risky investment because they want to be able to get their money back easily if the loan goes into default. Here are some other suggestions to get started:

- The quickest and most liquid funds are cash in the bank. Any cash sitting around earning less than 1% interest would be a great start.

- Any common stocks held in your name outside a qualified retirement plan can be converted to cash.

- I.R.A.s (Individual Retirement Plans) or Keogh plans. You can outright liquidate the plan or borrow against the balance when the plan allows for it. The advantage of this type of loan is that it's not taxable. Depending on the size of your retirement plan, this is a great way to jump-start your property acquisition. Most 401Ks will not allow participants to borrow more than 50% of the outstanding balance and a loan has to be paid back over a certain period of time. Be aware that if the amount is not paid back, the I.R.S. might consider it taxable income.

- Home equity loans and cashing out refinance loans. The banks are not making these loans as much today as in previous years, but they still exist and some people still qualify for them.

- Personal physical assets like gold and silver coins, or other collectible items that have value and can be converted to cash. Look around the house, garage, and shop. Have a huge garage sale or utilize Craigslist and other online sales forums.

- Personal line of credit with a bank or credit union. The amount of your line of credit will depend on several factors, including income, credit score, and the bank's regulations. Terms are usually for a period of 5-7 years, with monthly payments and interest based on the outstanding balance.

- Credit cards

- Hard money loans. Keep in mind that these rates are much higher than other loans, with less room for flexibility.

- Partnerships with other people willing to invest.

- Cash value in Whole life or Universal Life insurance plans. You may be able to access cash by liquidating the residual cash value in the plan or by taking a loan against the value.

- Federal and or state tax refunds. This is a great way to raise cash because your refund arrives in a big chunk, and that amount can be a great catalyst toward investing.

BARRIERS TO EFFECTIVE COMMUNICATION AND PARTNERSHIPS

There are many factors that create communication barriers between partners and between employers and employees that hinder performance. Let's explore some of these factors.

1. Past military ranking: Past military ranking does not translate into current or future ranking. A person may find themselves working for another whom they previously outranked in a prior military experience. It is a good idea to keep prior experiences and prior ranking to oneself. If you are young and your employer/contractor previously outranked you, it may be difficult for them to recognize and respect the change.

2. Age: Age will always be an issue. Whether you are the younger or older person, respect for the other is vital. Passing on experience and wisdom is important.

3. Family background: Many people's family backgrounds cause them to limit their business interactions to only friends and family members. To build and expand most businesses, it is required to work and communicate outside one's inner circle.

4. Religious preferences: Some people will only trust, work with, or hire people of the same faith. Without diminishing anybody's faith or belief system, it is important to keep to the business at hand and not allow our religious stereotypes to interfere with our rationale.

5. Educational experience: Many highly educated people believe they are smarter and more entitled to success and opportunities than anyone less educated. This mentality can interfere in a business transaction when a less formally educated but better informed person is in the driver's seat. This bias can be a serious roadblock for a highly educated person when they are not in command of a business relationship or must rely on others (who are more savvy) to perform certain functions.

6. Overall looks and mannerisms: Every person carries him or herself in a special and unique way. Self-awareness is important, and that each person is able to identify their own comfort level and persona.

Chapter 10

Purchasing Property From Sellers

Case Studies: Purchasing Property

Using your own cash

While looking over listings on the internet, you notice a 3 acre property located on the highway. You call the listing agent and she tells you that the property is an estate sale, meaning the original owner of the property died and their family is settling the estate. You look at the property in person and can tell it would make a great investment. The listed price is $7,000. You offer $5,000 and they counter at $5,500. Because you trust your intuition and know a good thing when you see it, you settle with the listing agent for $5,500. You have some money saved up from the last 2 years in an account, earning half of 1 percent interest, and decide to use it buy the property. You close in 3 weeks with a new property.

Cash and Borrowing

You find a piece of property on the internet being sold through a local real estate company for $18,000 cash. The property is 5 acres, with power and phone installed, on the highway. With a little research, you learn that the seller's father owned the land for twenty years and left it to her three years ago when he passed away. The seller doesn't want the property and the hassles of managing it, including the $120 a year in property taxes for land she doesn't visit. Due to family financial issues (unemployment, debt, etc.) she is eager to sell. Enter the investor, the problem solver. By buying this property as an investor, you are potentially making a profit while helping the seller and her family limit or even eliminate hassles.

Additionally, you notice the property has been on the MLS (Multiple Listing Service) for over 8 months, which may be the result of several things. It could be that the price is too high. Given that the agent used the assessor's numbers to value and price the land for listing, this is possible, because an assessor's land value is subjective. It may also indicate that buyers in the area aren't interested in land having only power and phone. Another good reason that the property has not sold might be that the seller is requesting cash and very few people have $18,000 in cash available for a semi-improved property an hour outside of town.

After consulting with your business partner, spouse, or real estate agent, you decide to place an offer on the property for $12,000 cash to close in 3 weeks. You don't have the $12,000 in the bank, but you do have $5,000 available from a Christmas present a parent gave you last year, and you know you can borrow the remaining $7,300 dollars (the additional $300 will be needed for buyer's closing costs) from your credit card cash line. The seller accepts the offer and the deal closes in 3 weeks.

Owner Financing with a small amount down

While talking with a local real estate agent, you ask if he knows any sellers who would be willing to sell on a contract with a small down payment. In other words, you are asking if he has any pocket listings. There are many reasons sellers will choose to sell on a contract instead of taking cash. They may want a monthly income and are willing to risk a buyer's default because they don't want the management hassles and costly property taxes each year.

The agent tells you about a 10 acre property, with power and phone on the corner of the land, that the seller has owned for years and is ready to let go of. The property does not have a listing price (as it is not listed) but the seller will take a price of $14,000 with $3,000 as a down payment. The seller is willing to finance the balance of $11,000 over 5 years at 7% interest, with monthly payments at $218 per month. After looking at the property, you decide that it has some potential. You quietly accept the price and terms of the property. You pay a little bit more of the closing costs, as the agent has to make a commission.

100% FINANCING

While looking in the Sunday newspaper ads, you notice a small ad that reads '11 acres for sale.' The advertised price is $18,000. You call because you are familiar with the area and ask a few questions. Good questions include: Why are you selling? How long have you owned the property?

The seller tells you he is moving far outside of the area and has no intentions of coming back. This is a hint to you that he wants to unload the property. Furthermore, he has owned the property over 20 years and has not done much to improve it, nor has he visited the property a lot. At this point, you are more than curious but still a little apprehensive and decide to meet him on the property to look it over.

At the property, you notice a few big trees that have probably been there for over 25 years. You offer the seller $14,000 cash to close in 2 weeks. He needs the money for moving expenses and agrees quickly.

You have the $14,000 but don't want to use it, because you believe there is at least $10,000 in marketable timber on the property. This means that only $4,000 is at risk. You call your silent money partner, better known as a hard money lender, and ask if he wants in. He gives you the money for a 50% equity, and you close in 2 weeks. Keep in mind, if you did not have the $14,000 cash in hand or a hard money partner, there are still other ways to finance the deal. Bank loans, borrowing from relatives, utilizing internet peer to peer lending, borrowing through credit cards, etc. can all be a start. 100% financing means that no money out of your pocket.

CHAPTER 11

Good Situations for Selling Land on Owner Terms or Contracts

THERE WILL ALWAYS BE PROBLEMS, issues, and unpredictable scenarios confronting someone selling on owner or contract terms. The dialogue here is not an attempt to address all possible situations, but will shed light on some of the more common issues. For these and many other problems, there is a remedy.

SELLING SCENARIO 1

You own a piece of property next to a homeowner's property and their son wants to purchase the land to be next to his parents. The son doesn't have a good down payment (a 'good' down payment is anything in the area of 10% of the purchase price or higher).

The best solution is to sell the land as a 'lease to purchase.' The purchase price is $10,000, making the down payment $2,000. You agree to collect $200 per month from the son for 10 months, applying this amount towards the down payment, and then sell to him on a contract for the remaining $8,000. Problem solved. The son is able to live close to his family, and you receive a monthly income stream. This is win-win for all parties.

SELLING SCENARIO 2

You are selling a property and while the potential purchasers have a good consistent income, they do not have a large amount of money for a down payment. They want to develop the land gradually with their own money on their own time as they slowly collect the necessary funds, and you want a monthly income stream.

In this situation, you and the purchaser enter a sort of loose partnership. You agree to sell to them on contract, knowing that as they make improvements, they will have increasing incentive to make timely payments to you and to not default. You gain from this because the property is improved without cost to you. Both sides benefit.

SELLING SCENARIO 3

The potential purchaser for a piece of land you are selling has no money for capital improvements and can only make very minimal monthly payments. Because of these factors, you decide not to sell the land and rent it out instead. You make the capital improvements in your own time frame and to your own discretion while collecting monthly land rental payments.

When the improvements are finished, you will be able to sell to the purchaser on an owner contract, but with a higher price because the improvements make it more valuable, useable, and in demand. Once again, the purchaser is getting an improved property with no costs or risks to him. You receive monthly payments during the improvement period and a higher payment when the improvements are done. This is win-win.

Chapter 12

Possible Outcomes of Selling Land on Contract

A WHOLE BOOK COULD BE WRITTEN on the potential outcomes of seller financed contracts, but I will limit my the focus here to the advantages to the seller. People who have never sold a property on contract will not at first understand the dynamics of this, but with continued experience you will come to understand the complexities.

I believe the best place to start in this discussion is to define the ideal buyer—this is one who buys on a contract, pays on time every month and pays off the note on time, according to the contract terms (which could range from a few years to several decades). I have found that only a small percentage, usually 20-50%, of buyers pay on time. If you have ten accounts, this equates to between 2 to 5 people paying on time, like clock work. We can acknowledge most people would say this isn't a very good record.

How can somebody build a reliable source of cash flow with those odds? This is a good question for another book, but here I will only say that it is important not to be over-leveraged, especially in the beginning of a business. More specifically, if you have ten properties and have sold all ten on contract, it would be prudent to have at least 3 to 5 of these be mortgage free. Ideally, it would be better to have all ten be mortgage free, without any underlying costs to pay.

When beginning a business, it is better to build up several properties free and clear of any mortgages or deeds of trust. When one has several of these types of properties, then prudent and responsible leverage of properties is possible and encouraged, and will increase your total return.

Now, there are several possibilities and outcomes when selling land on a real estate contract. We will discuss a few good outcomes here.

As discussed earlier, some people who want to sell land on contract think the best course is to buy low and sell high. These people imagine they will buy a piece of land for $20,000, spend $10,000 in improvements, and then sell for $50,000, making $20,000 in profit. Although this does happen, I have found that with rural residential properties, cash outs are rare.

The first good outcome when selling on contract would be having a buyer pay off the note early, mainly in the first 2-5 years. Depending on the terms of the contract in this situation, a seller earns a little in interest and a lot in capital gain if the selling price is higher than the cost of the property. However, if you are trying to build a monthly income selling land on contract, this outcome is not ideal unless you are able to roll the cash proceeds in another better property or more valuable group of properties. Of all the properties I have sold, this outcome has occurred less than 10% of the time. When it does occur, it's very important to have a strategy for utilizing the cash out funds. Without proper planning, these funds have a tendency to dissipate.

A second good outcome occurs when a buyer gets behind in their payments and either 'Quit Claims' the property back to the seller or a seller has to foreclose or forfeit the buyer.

A third ideal outcome for a seller occurs when a buyer goes the full number of years on the note. In my experience, this outcome rarely happens, occurring only 10-20% of the time.

Chapter 13

Traits Needed to Succeed in the Land Business

Desire

WHAT DO YOU DESIRE? Freedom? Independence?

A long-time loyal employee who is suddenly laid off from a job will have a strong desire to financially support his family. He or she may develop a strong desire to prove to their former employers that they can better themselves. Someone anticipating that they will be without work in 6 months or so will also develop a desire to plan ahead to support his or her family, developing a sense of urgency A desire to overcome adversity is also a strong motivator—whether it be rising above a disability, memories of childhood bullying, or a tough family environment—as is wanting to move up in the world, beyond a mediocre beginning. The pain of these things can be deep and continue to hurt, putting a fire in your belly to succeed.

The point is that we all have reasons behind a desire to succeed and better ourselves. We have to dig deep, realize it, and remember it. It starts with our inner being and flows outward from there. Once we realize it, we must also not have too many distractions from our goal. Many things in life are distracting and we can't allow them to hold us back from marching on to better ourselves.

Humility

This trait starts with your mother, father, or grandparents telling you to say 'thank you,' 'please,' and 'hello.' This trait practices and improves on good etiquette toward other people, allowing you to win with a somber attitude and without seeming brash and cocky. It involves losing with grace and congratulating your opponent. It involves treating everybody with kindness and respect, no matter what the circumstances. Regardless of how other people are acting or reacting in a situation, in the end it is how you treat *them* that really matters. More times than not, it is also what the other person will remember about you.

We also have to maintain a balance and not be too hard on ourselves when things are not going well, or if a sale doesn't work out like we thought it would. When I first started my business, I showed an older couple a nice property that I thought for sure they were going to buy. After spending 2 hours with them, they had told so many lies I was exhausted and confused. I hadn't realized people can lie so many times in such a short time. After becoming frustrated and blaming myself, I was eventually able to sell this same property to another buyer a few months later. This new buyer became one of my best customers, and also gave me an important referral which led to a very important sale. When things aren't going well, it's very easy to get frustrated, confused, and become willing to quit. But after this experience, I understood humility more, not because the end result was fine, but because the process encouraged me.

Persistence, Patience, 'People'

The third 'trait' we'll explore here is really a combination of three traits. Independent of each other, these qualities are good to have, but as a collective sum they are essential to not only short term but (more importantly) long term success. I like to call this combination 'being persistently patient with people.'

If you did a mental search of people close to you, whether from your family, your working relationships, or any ongoing one-on-one relationship, many people would have at least one of these traits. Although being able to get along with all kinds of people is critical, persistence and patience are just as important, if not more. Many extremely extroverted, fun loving people, fail in these other categories. This is a shortfall because of what is lacking in specific application. Alternately, many people have great persistence and patience, but are socially awkward and don't have a tolerance for different types of behavior and are easily rattled. Consider someone like a cool headed military sniper who is motivated and thorough but can't stand to be around people. To be successful, you need all three qualities.

We all have strengths and weaknesses. Know your strengths. Identify your weaknesses and work on those. Work twice as much on your weaknesses as you do on your strengths. The strengths are natural to you, so polish and refine them while you improve your weaknesses.

Seizing the Moment

It would be difficult to write a book like this without mentioning the concept of 'seizing the moment.' Many good motivational books exist that describe the certain steps needed to accomplish this or that goal. These books present 3, 5, 7, or 10 step programs. Some writers will say goal setting is important, while others claim it's not really relevant. I believe that it is. I have personally seen goal setting accomplish many things, and believe good systems are more successful than just good products because a good product is only one piece of a system.

I am writing about *action*. You must take action to make action. Without placing an ad on the internet or in print media, or putting a sign on a property, prospective clients won't know about the property being sold. Without writing a letter to a property owner, asking to buy his or her property, you will miss out on a good deal. If we get greedy and hold out for unfair terms, we can't get referrals from satisfied customers. Without proper patience shown to a long term client who gets behind in payments, we lose a referral. Without placing an offer to buy, applying for loans, and reselling, we won't receive cash flow. Business begets more business.

About the Author

Nicholas W. Maslaney was born and raised in Pittsburgh, and graduated with a B.S. in Accounting with a minor in Economics from Indiana University of Pennsylvania. Maslaney deployed on three ships with the U.S. Navy, and is a Desert Shield/Storm veteran, having served aboard the U.S.S. Niagara Falls (AFS-3) during the 1990-1991 campaign. He began investing in real estate in 1991, when he purchased his first 40 acres in Okanogan, Washington. He met his wife, Barbara, in September of that same year, and was married fifteen months later. He and Barbara have been happily married ever since. Maslaney left the Navy in 1998 and began investing in real estate full time at the start of 2003. He currently lives in western Washington.

Contact: land4all75@gmail.com

Facebook: www.facebook.com/nicholas.maslaney

CPSIA information can be obtained
at www.ICGtesting.com
Printed in the USA
LVOW13s0235080217
523549LV00006B/524/P